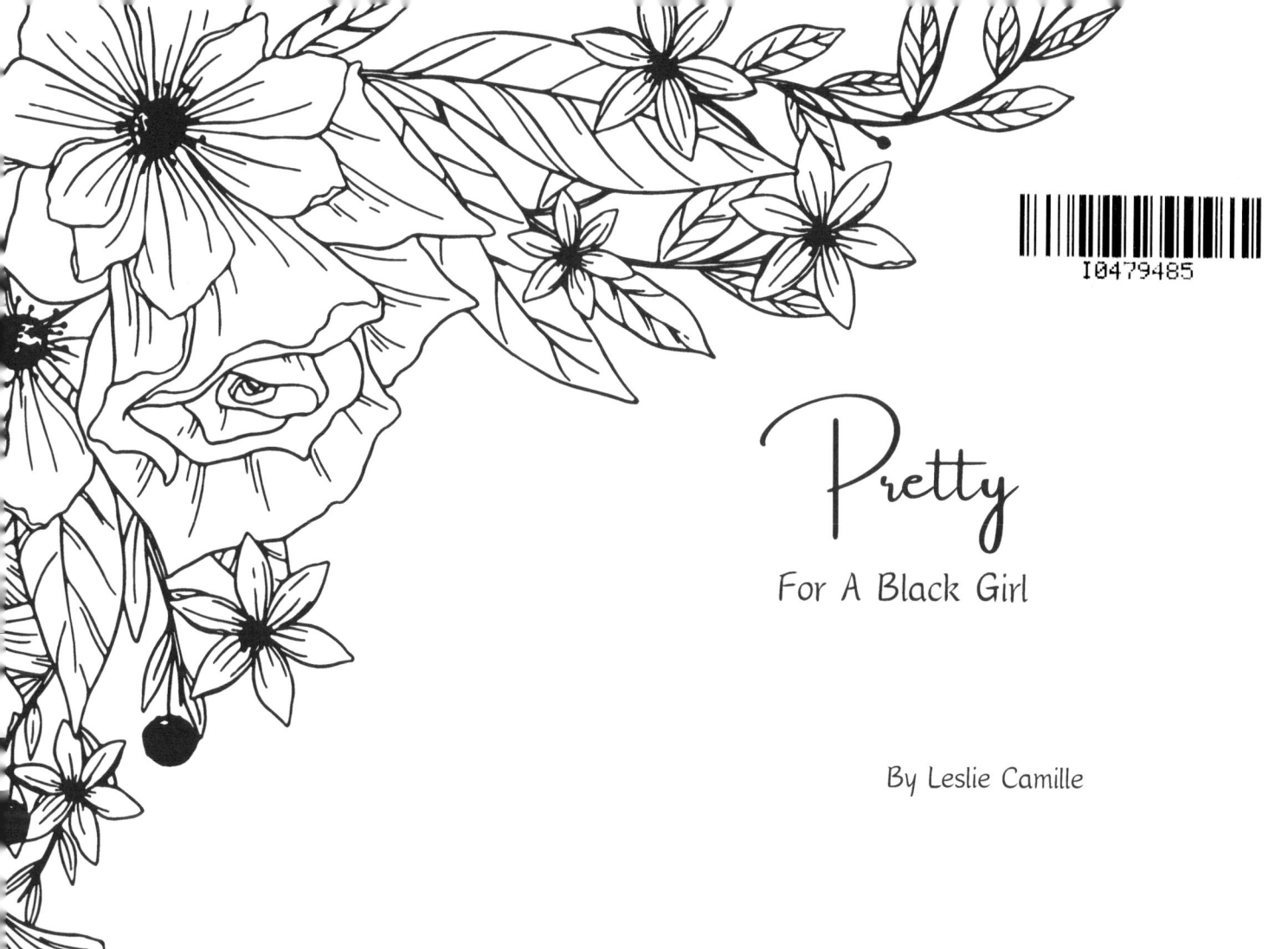

Pretty

For A Black Girl

By Leslie Camille

I0479485

This Book Belongs To:

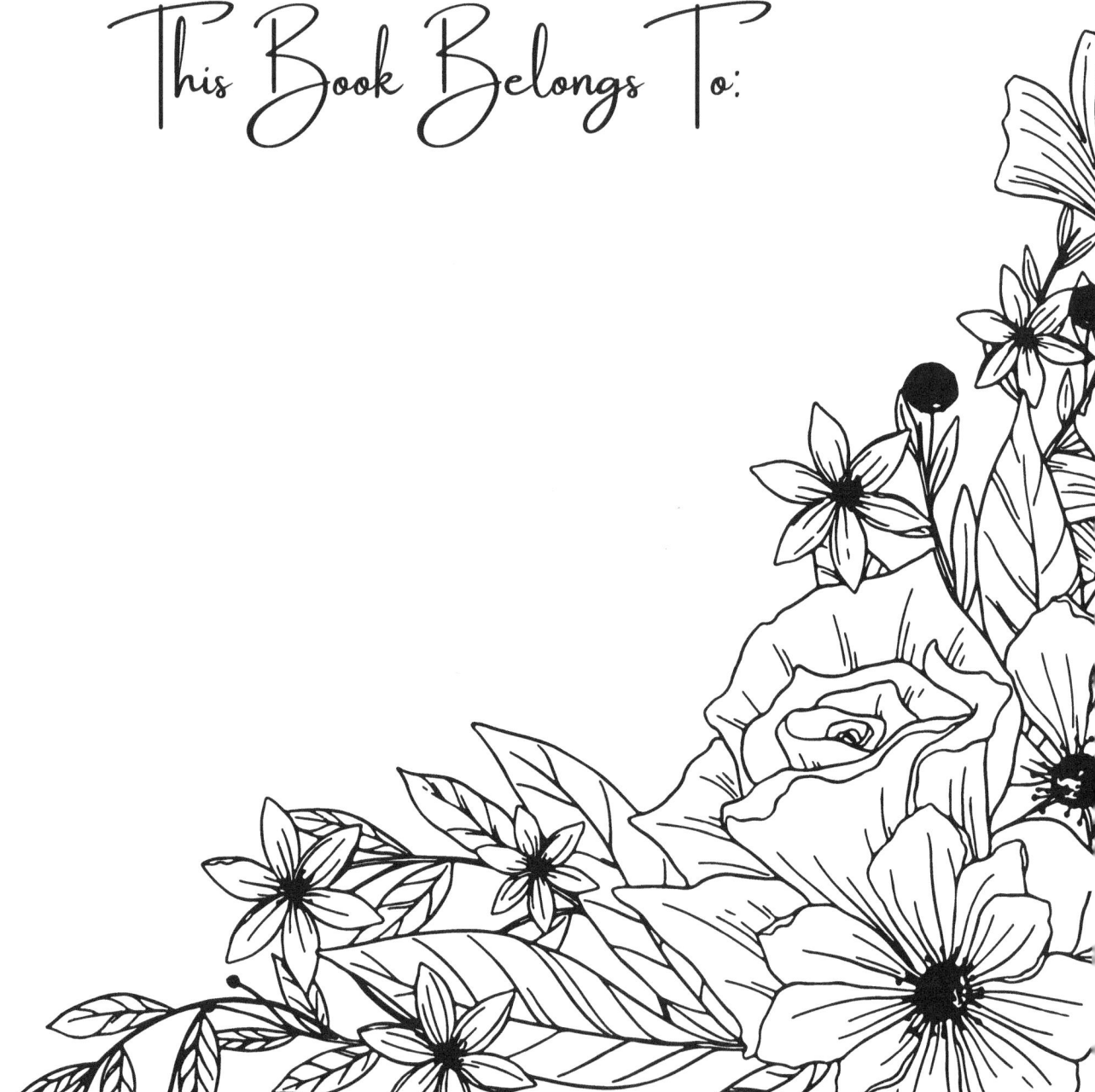

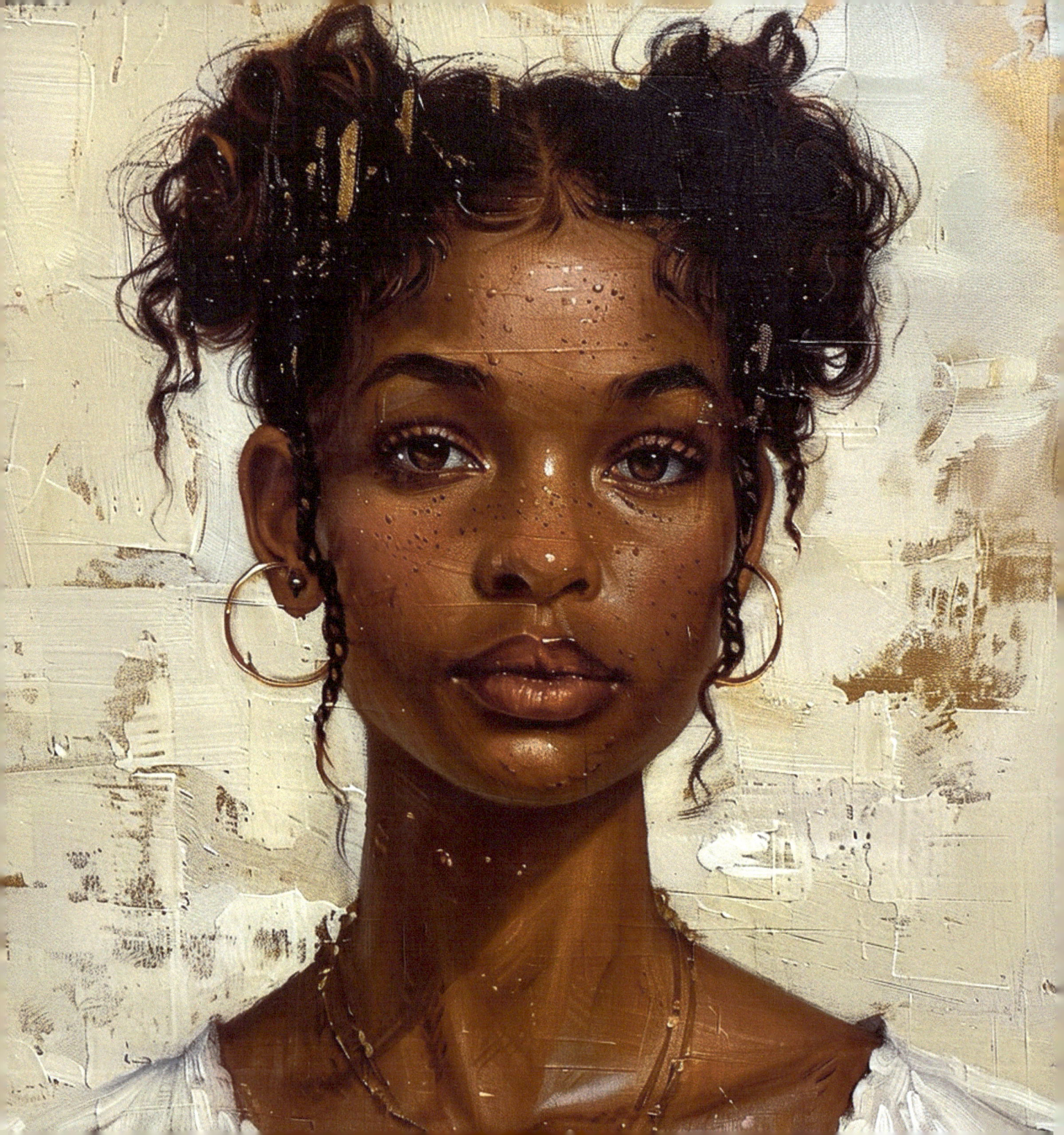

Brown eyes shine bright

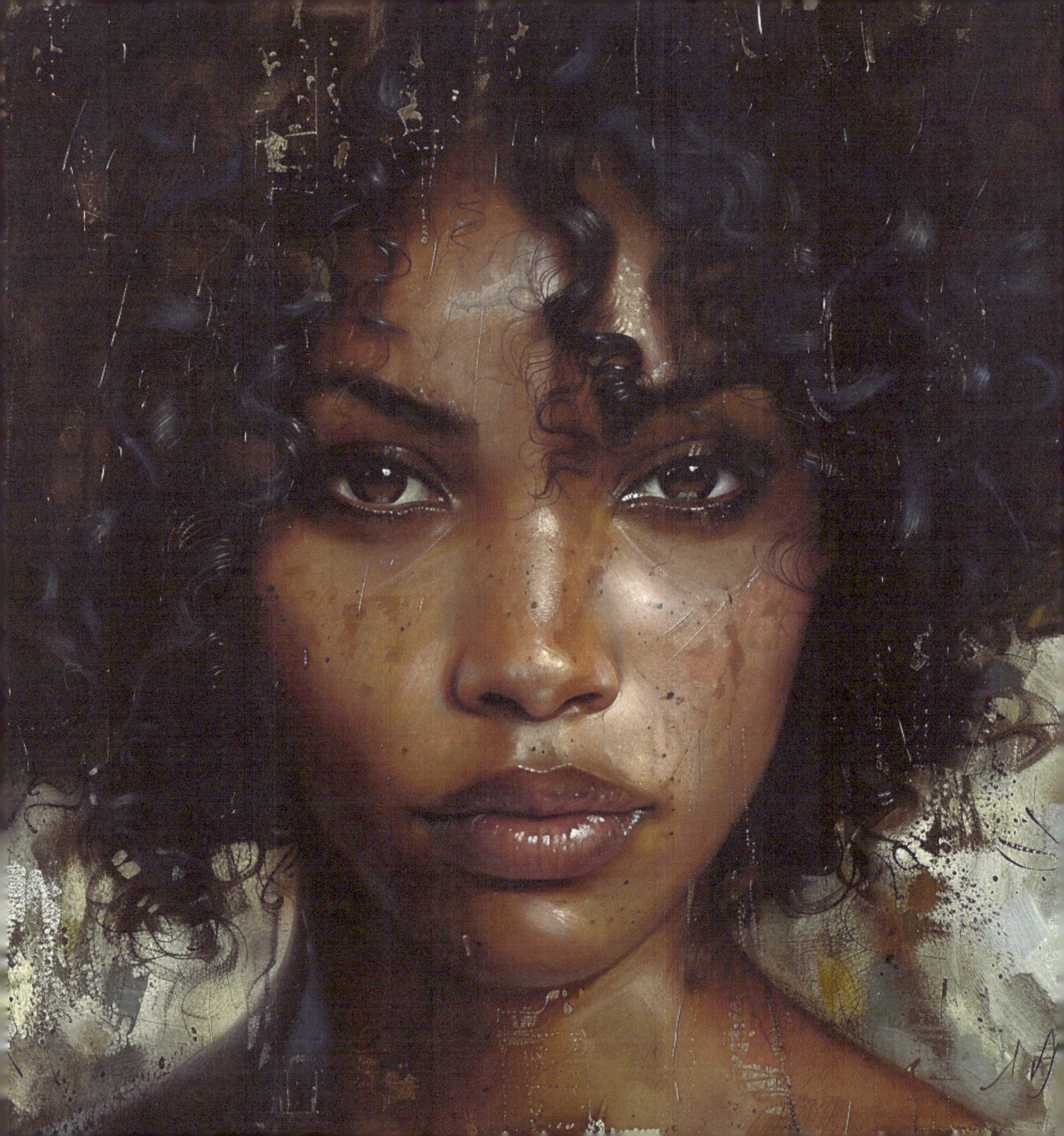

A crown of curls

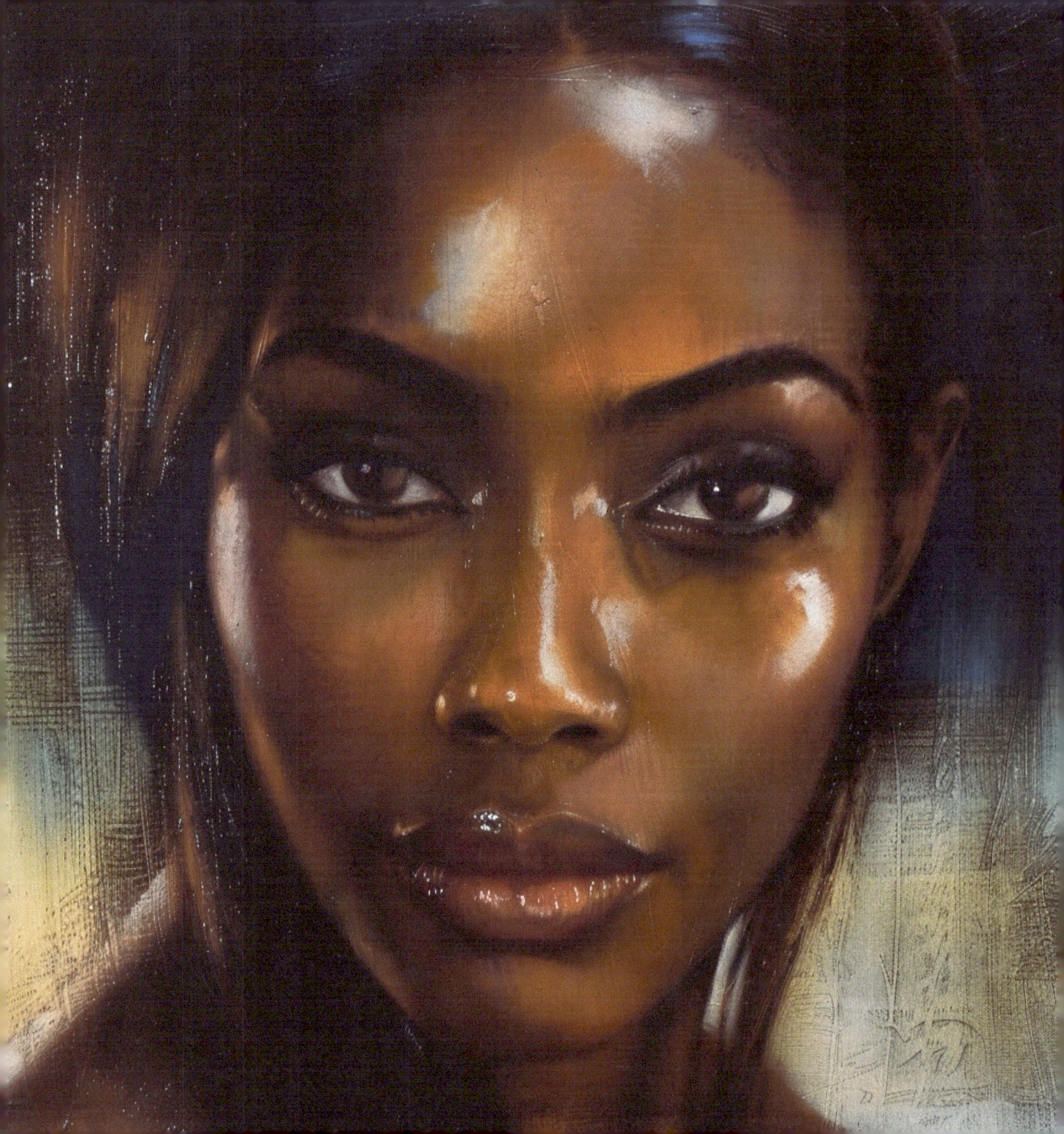

Full lips that smile

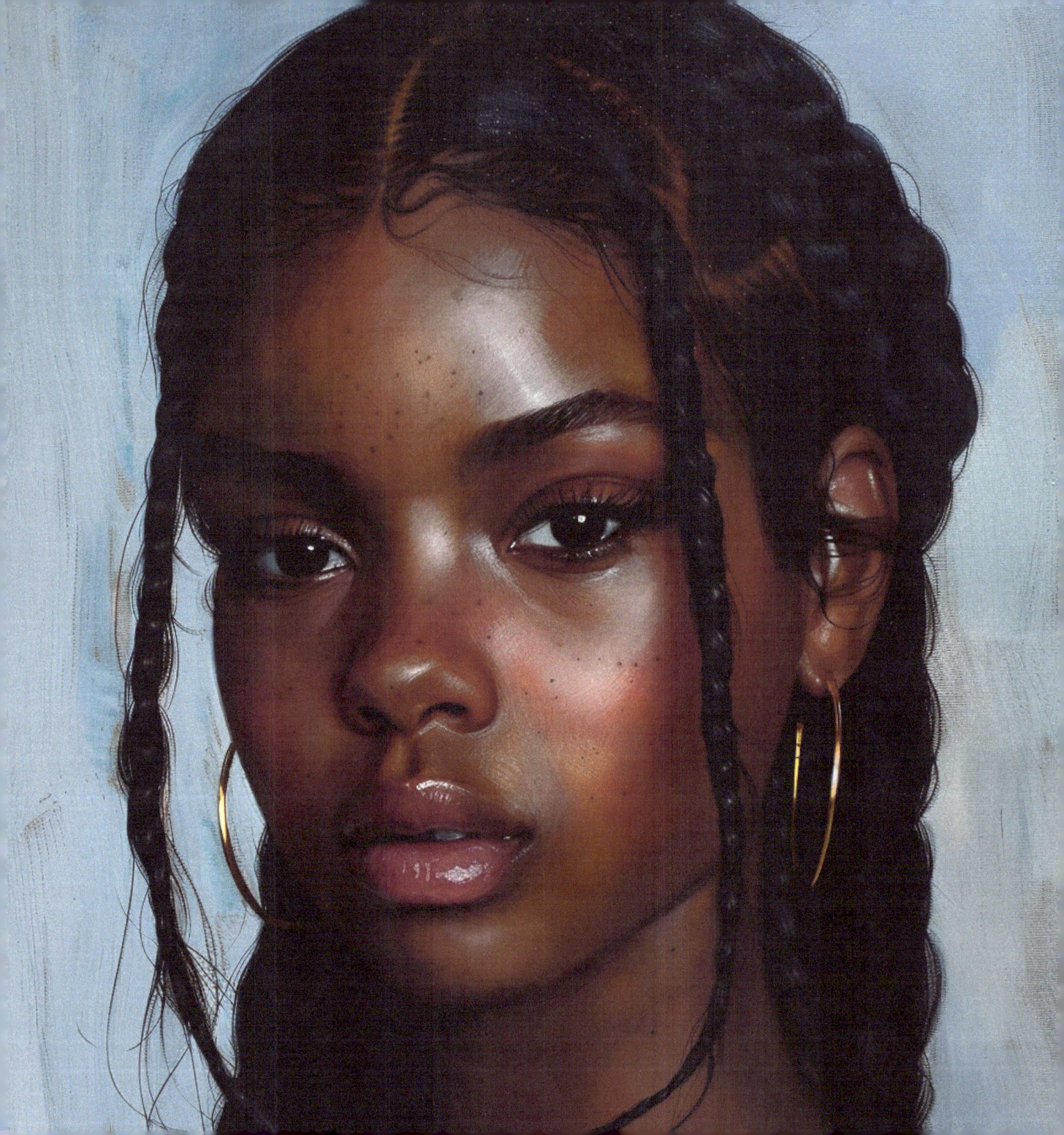

Dispelling all

the world's twirls

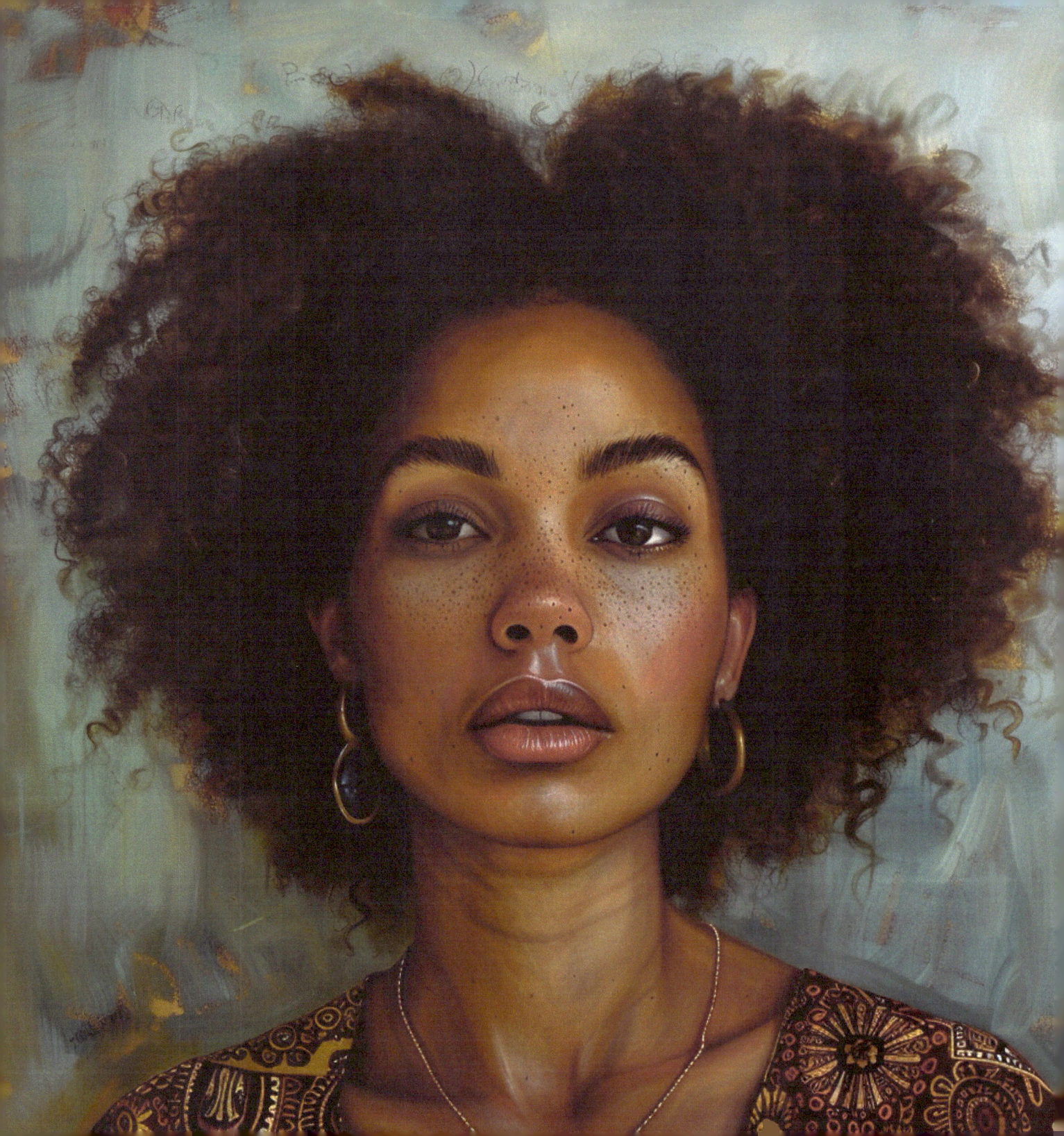

Freckles like stars

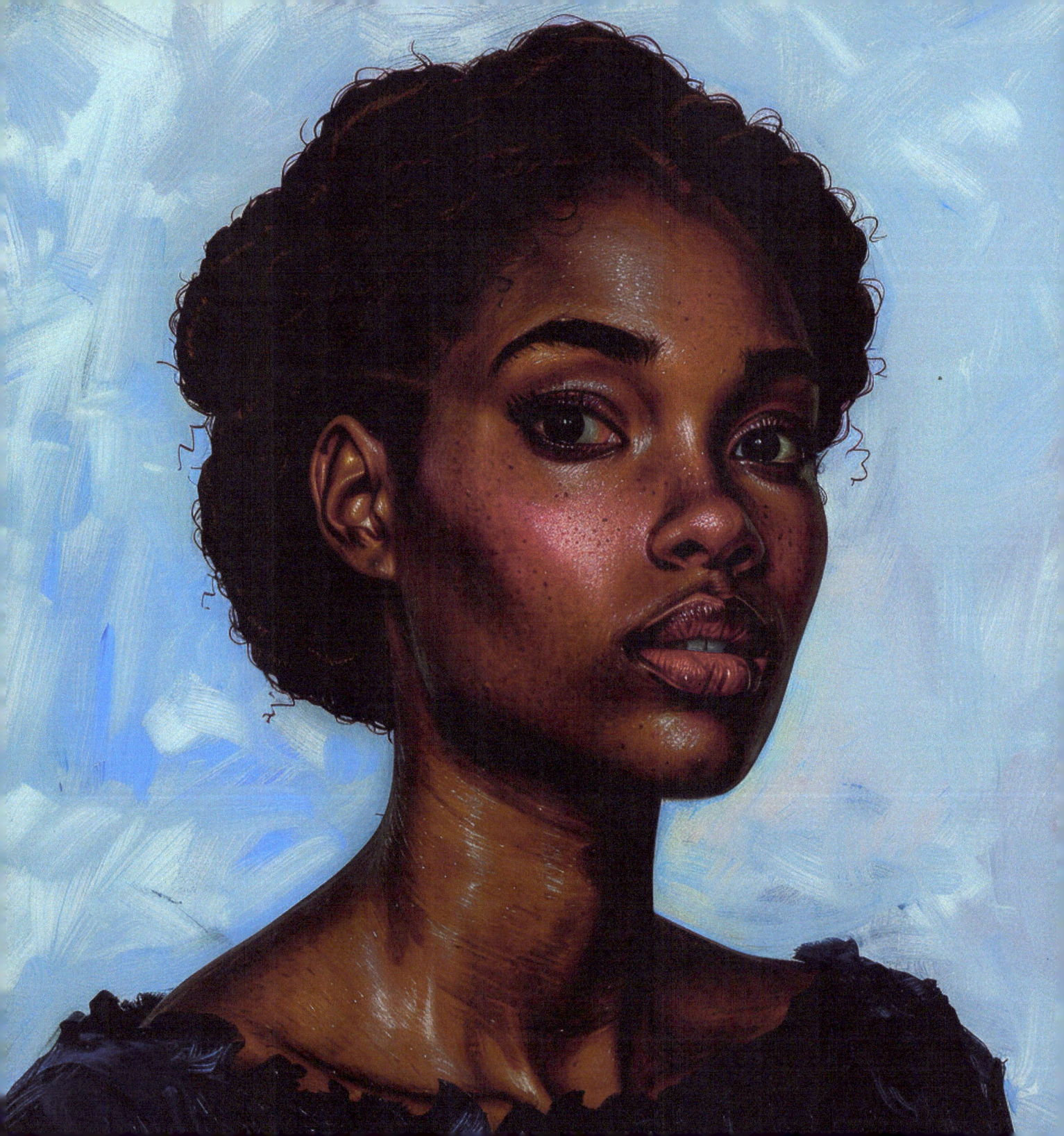

A canvas so unique

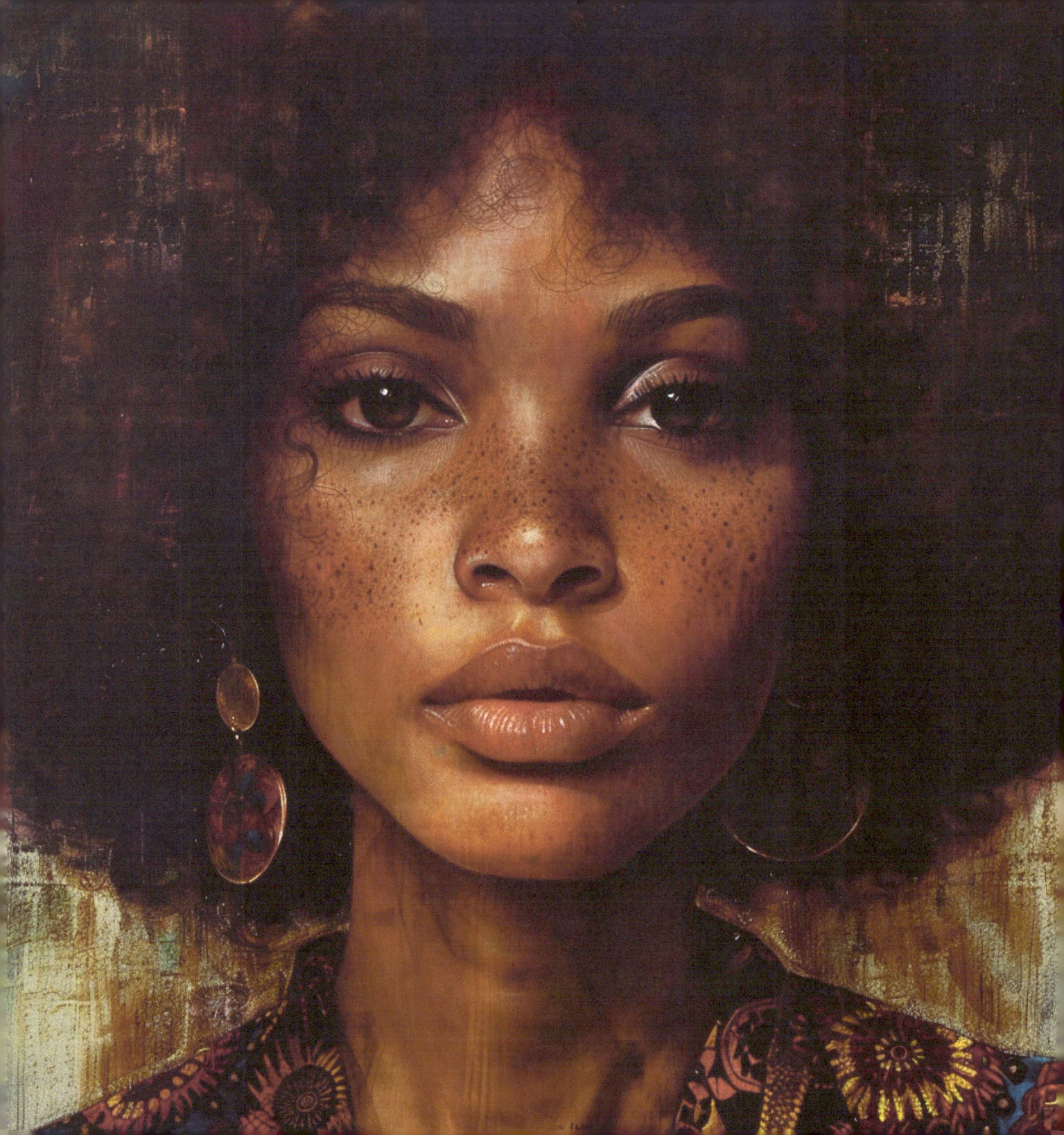

Every part of me,

beautiful and sleek.

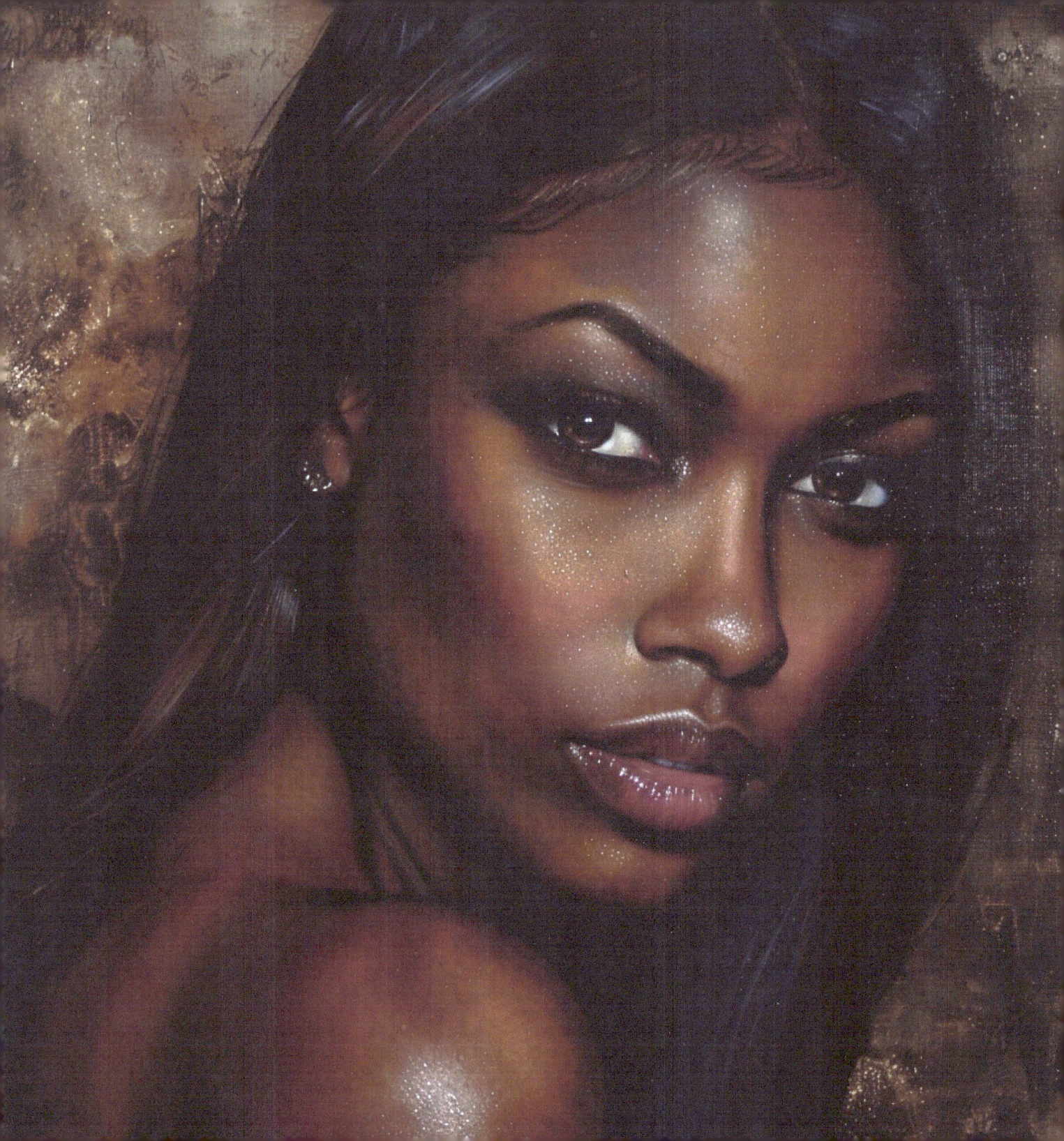

My skin, a rich hue,

like no other seen,

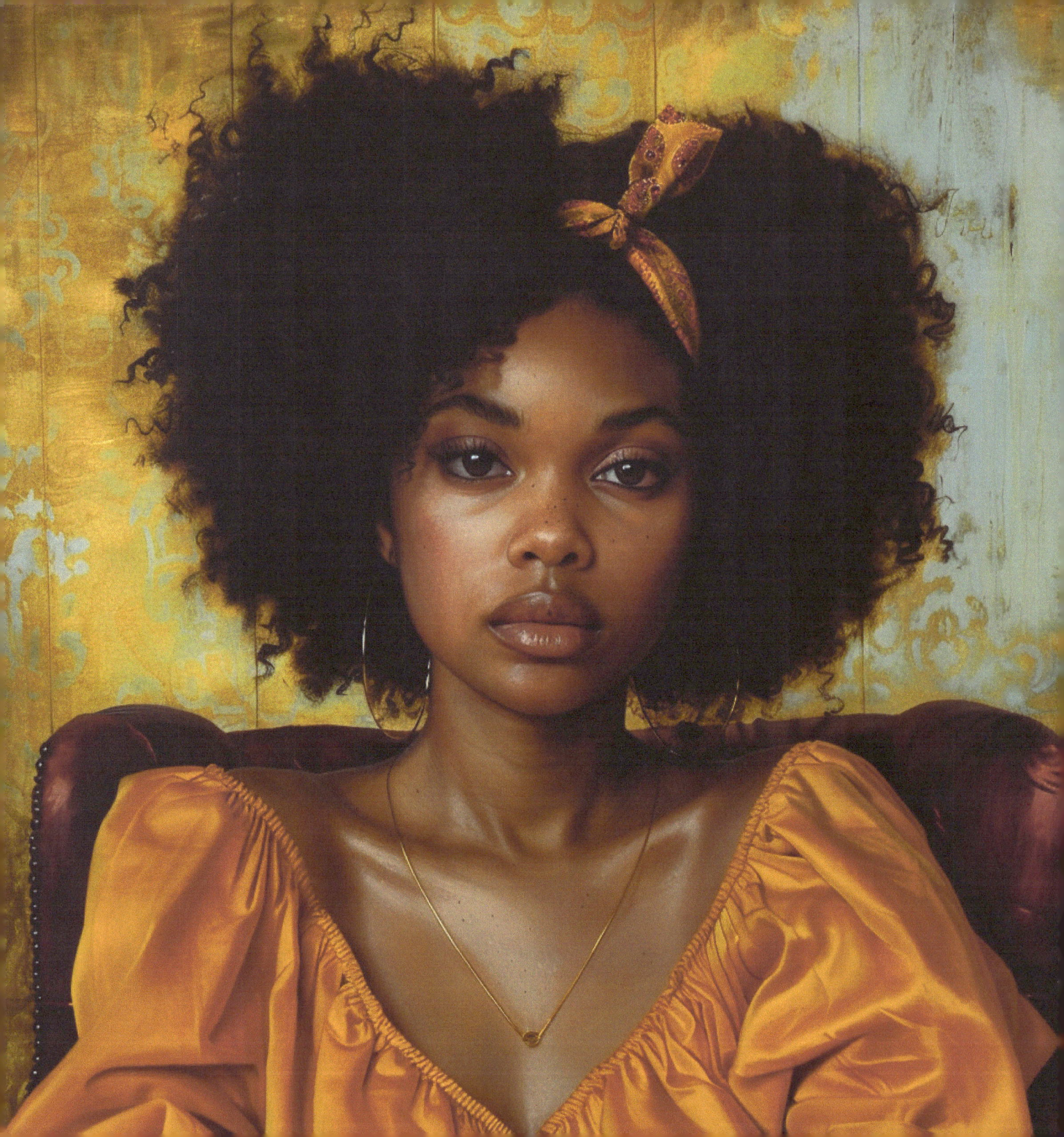

Art in human form,

a captivating queen.

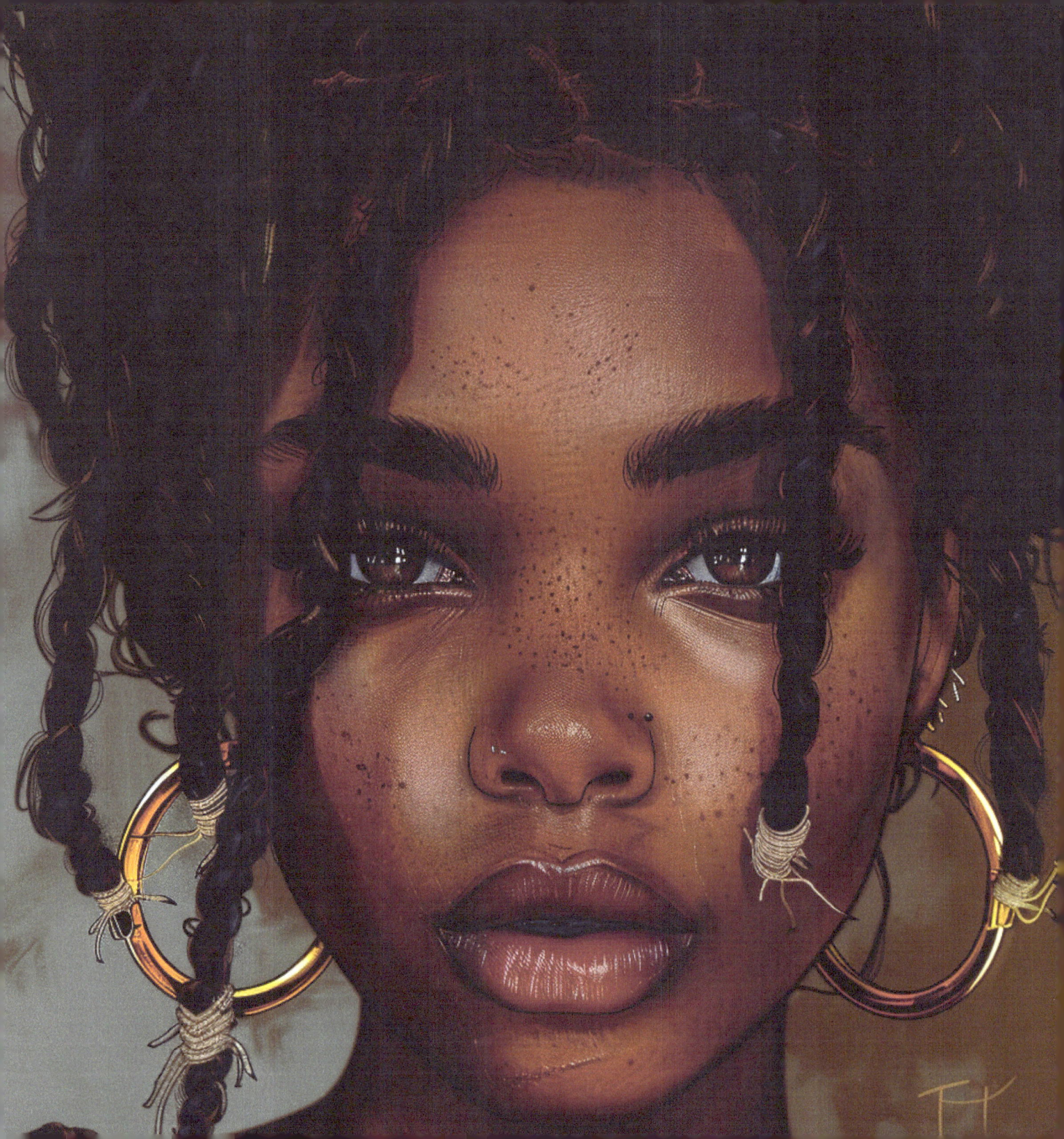

My movements, a poem,

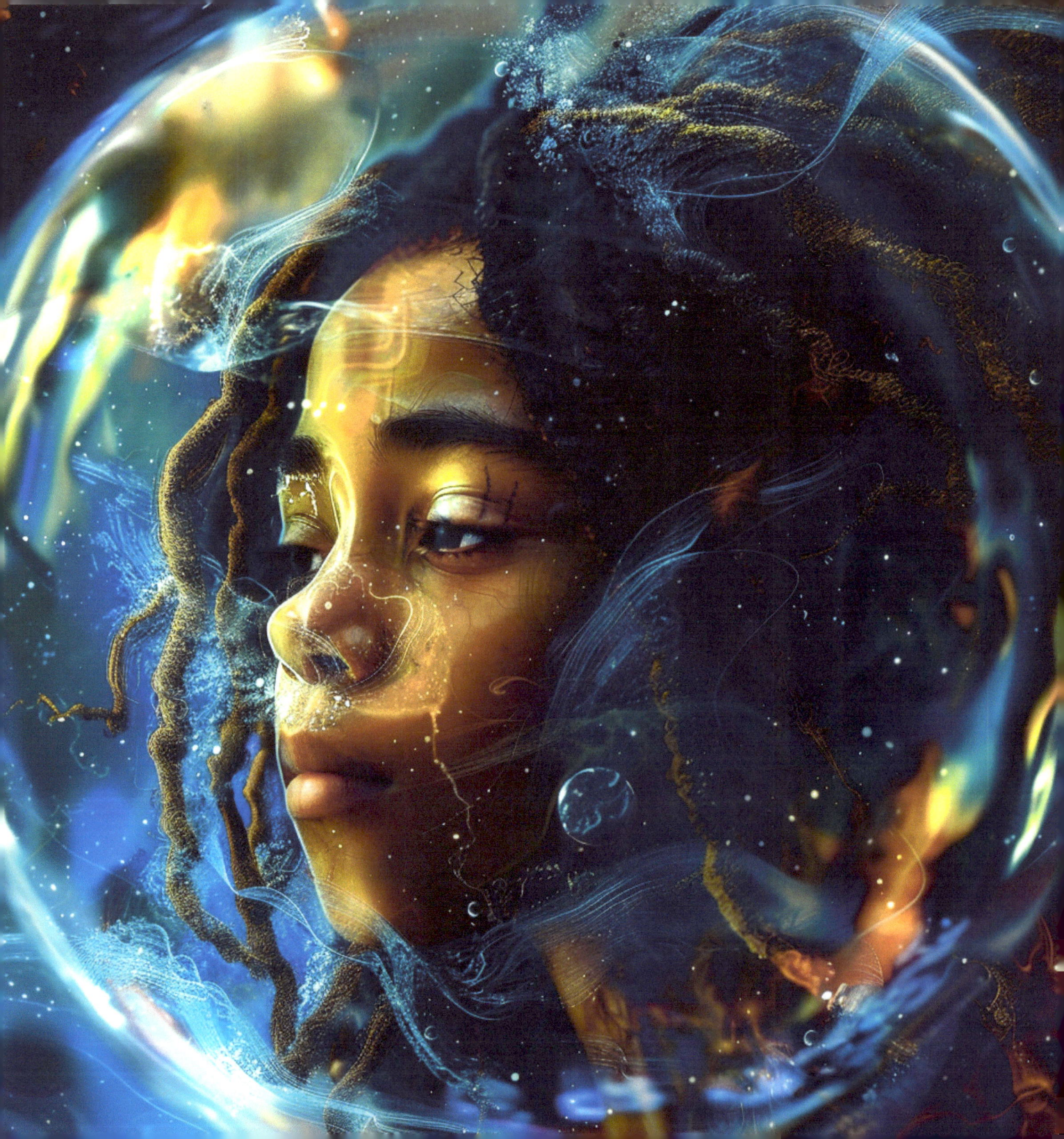

a story untold,

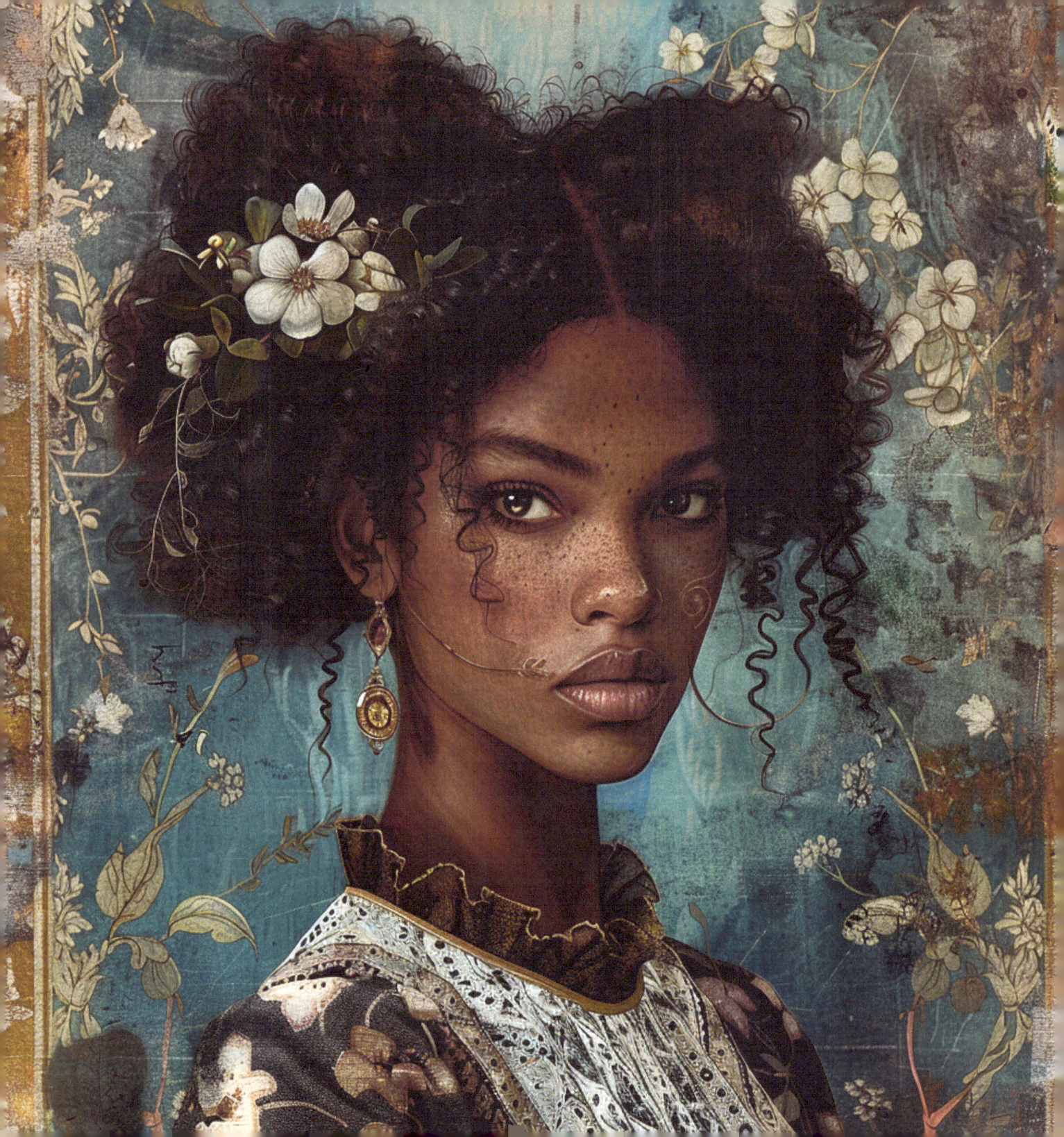

Like flowers in bloom,

brave, beautiful, and bold.

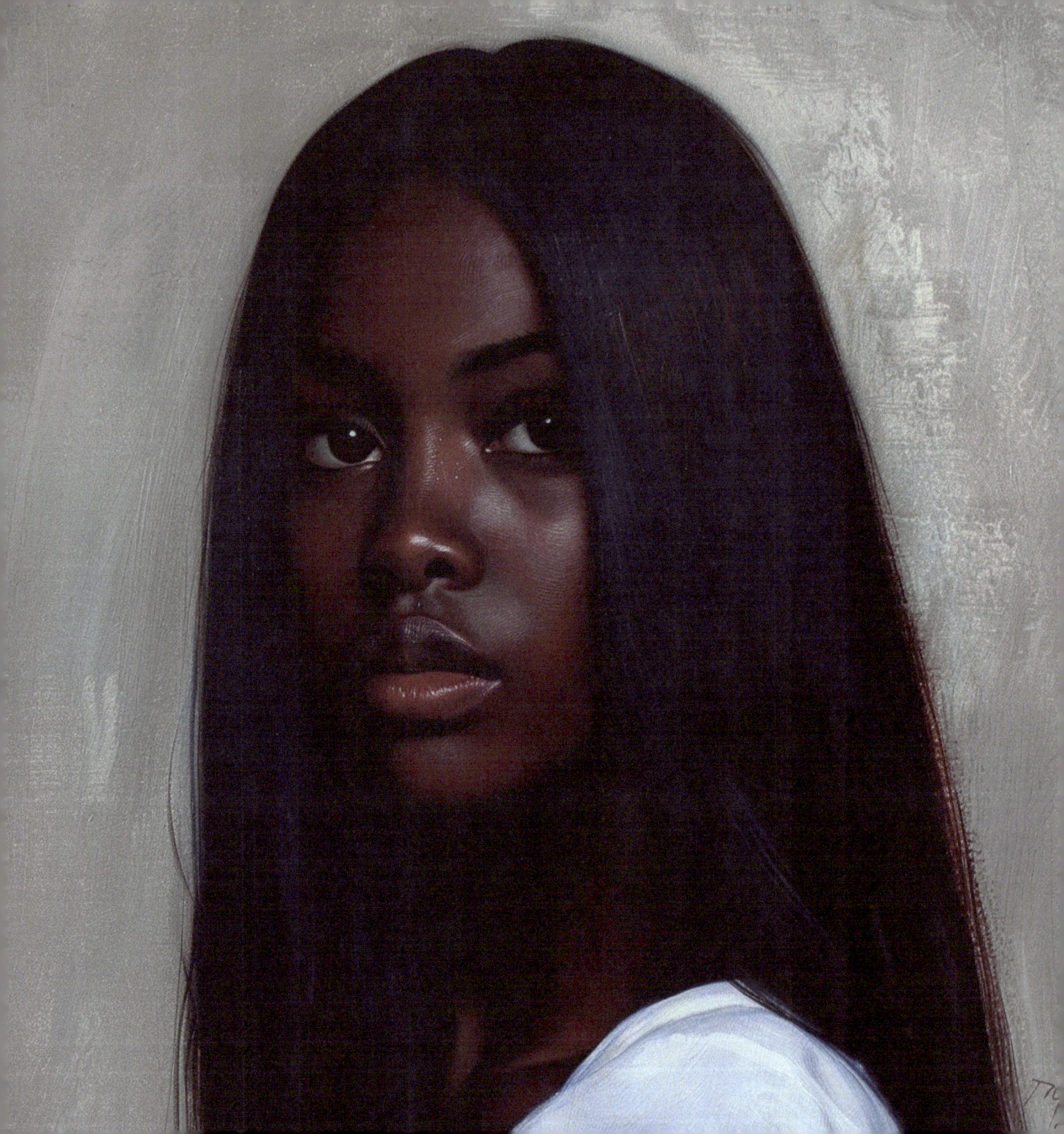

Regal and poised,

my spirit takes flight,

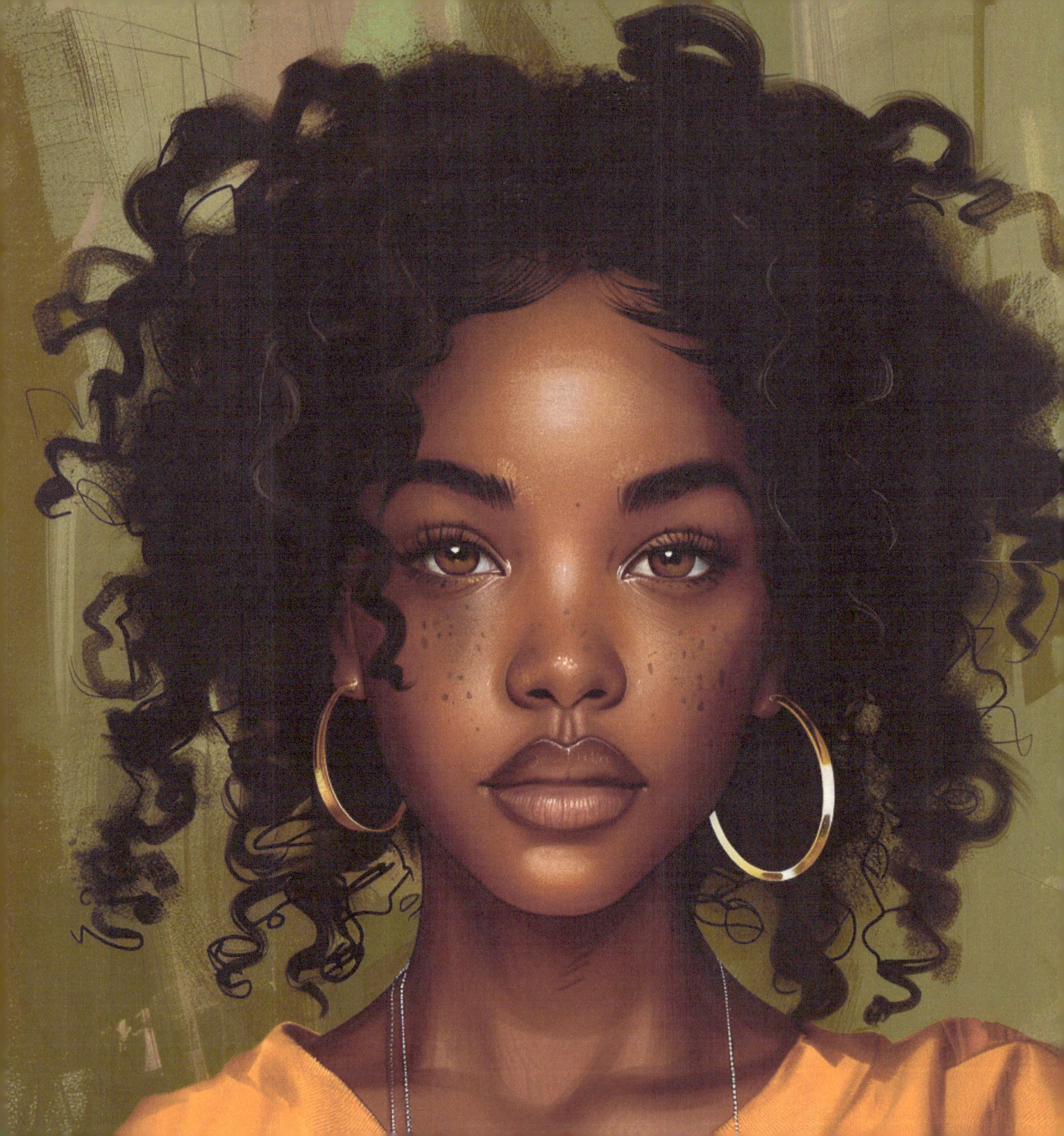

My colors ignite,

a radiant light.

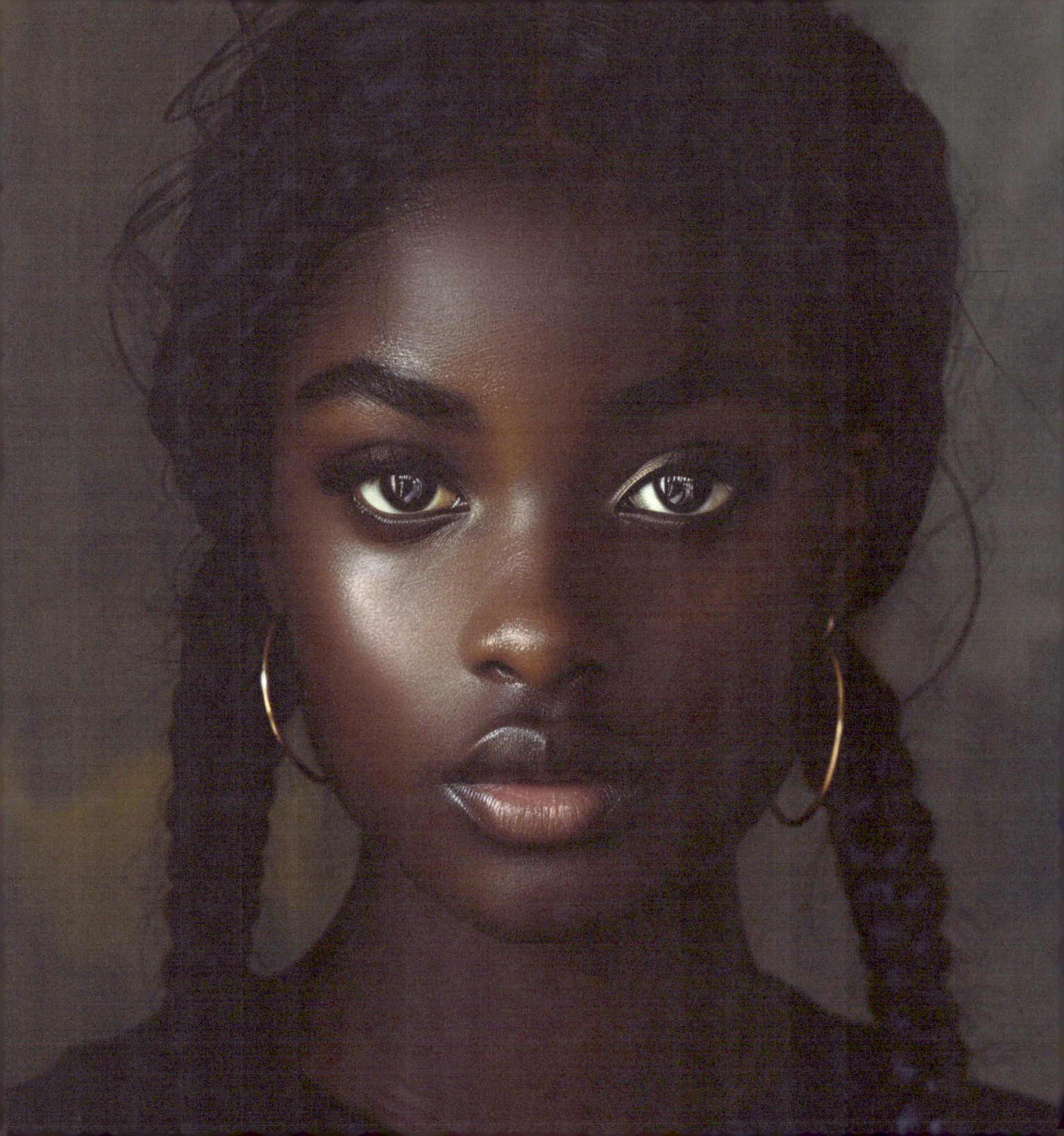

From Heaven and Earth,

my strength I claim.

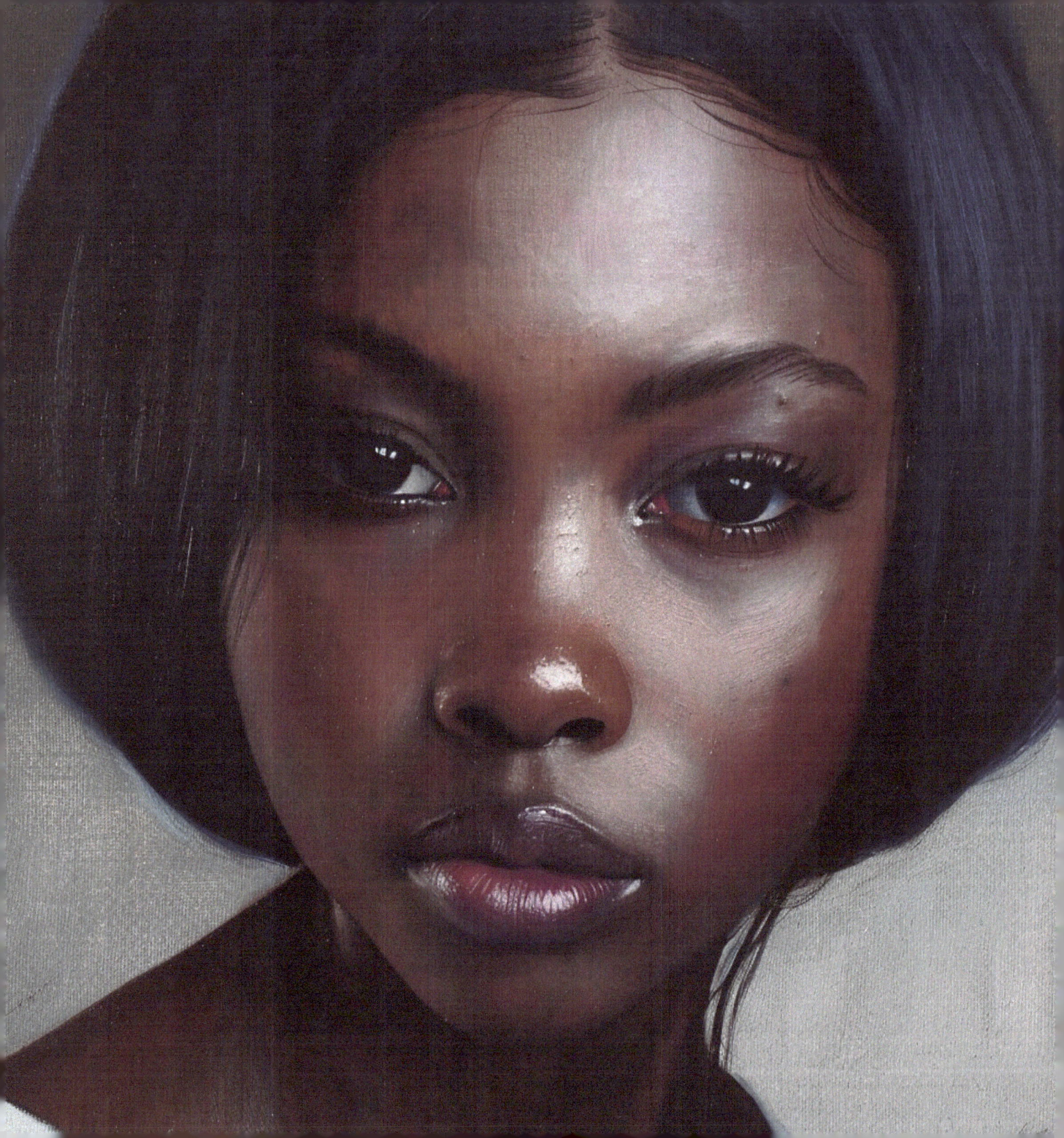

With the power of stars,

I rise above the flames.

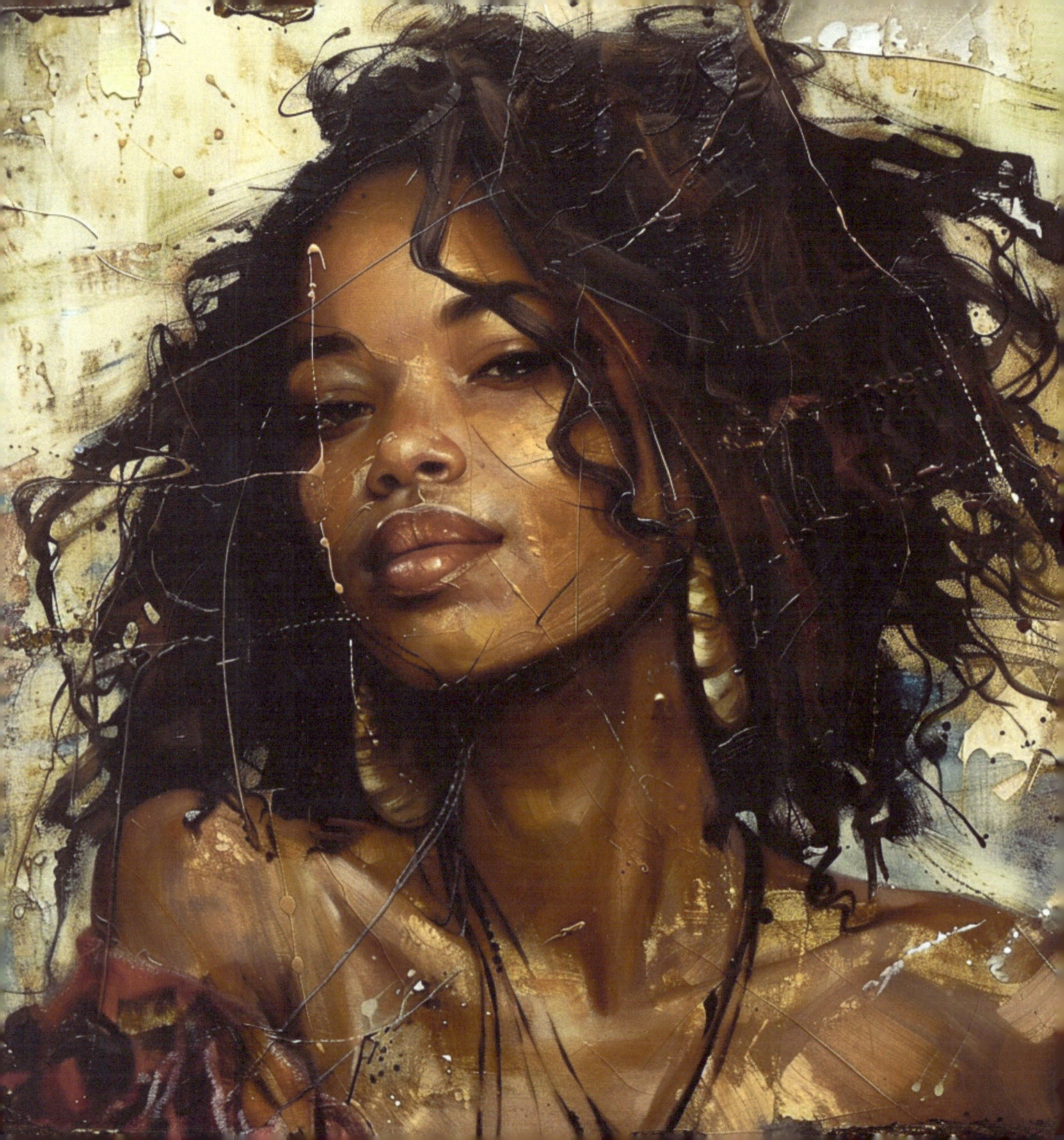

Black or white,

it matters not a bit,

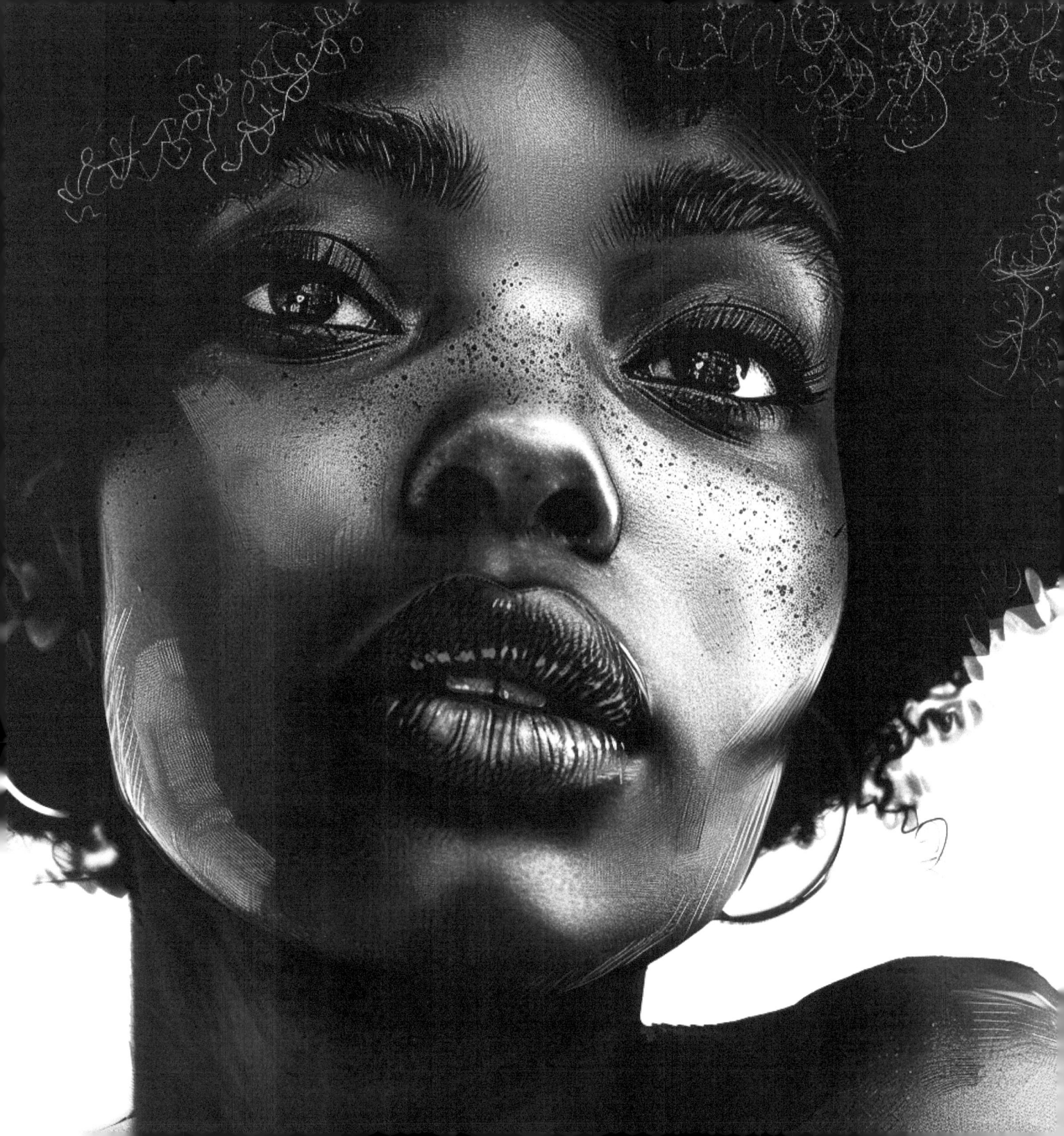

For in my own skin,

true beauty I emit.

Afterword

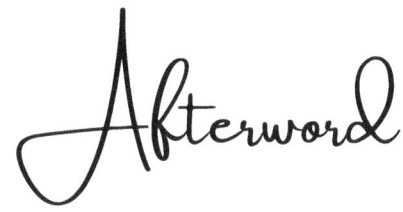

As you turn the final page, I hope this book has ignited a spark of joy and pride within you.

Being a woman or girl of color is a gift, a tapestry woven with vibrant cultures, rich histories, and unwavering strength.

These pages showcase a glimpse of that beauty, from the crown of curls to the spirit that shines like a radiant star. But remember, this celebration extends far beyond the last line.

The true magic lies in embracing every part of yourself — the laughter lines crinkling around your eyes, the way your hair defies definition, the fire in your heart that speaks volumes.

You are a masterpiece, a symphony of resilience and beauty.

The world needs your voice, your stories, your unique perspective. Let this book be a constant reminder to carry yourself with confidence, celebrate your heritage, and chase your dreams with unwavering determination.

You are worthy. You are powerful. You are beautiful,

not just "for" a woman or girl of color, but simply because you are you.

Carry this celebration with you, every single day. The world awaits your brilliance.

With love and admiration,

Leslie Camille

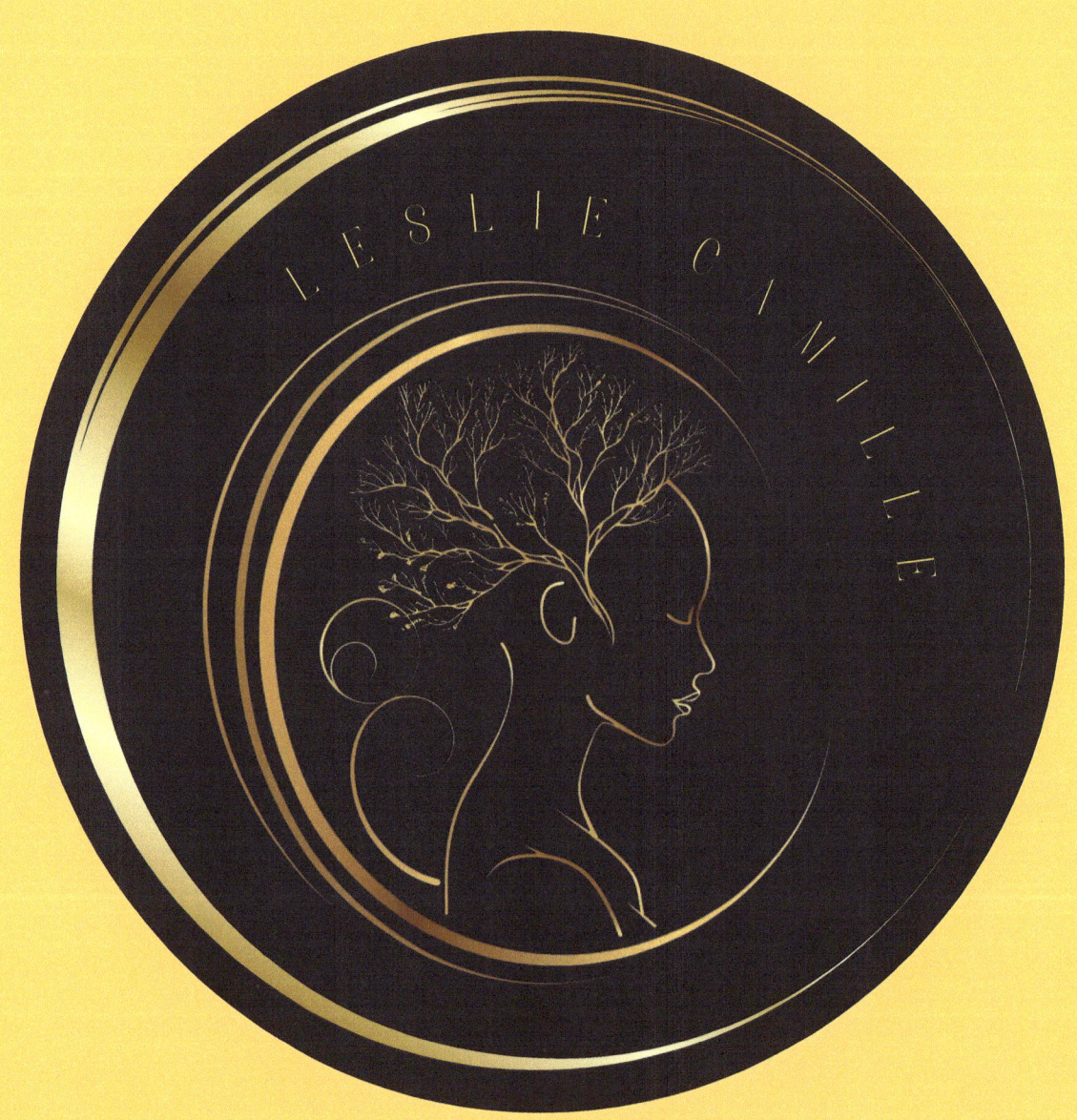

LESLIE CAMILLE

Copyright 2024

www.ingramcontent.com/pod-product-compliance
Lightning Source LLC
Chambersburg PA
CBHW042028230526
45474CB00006B/40